Transportation & Communication Series

Trucks and Big Rigs

Arlene Bourgeois Molzahn

Enslow Publishers, Inc.

40 Industrial Road
Box 398
Berkeley Heights, NJ 07922
USA

PO Box 38
Aldershot
Hants GU12 6BP
UK

http://www.enslow.com

With love to my grandson, Jack, who has shared his island with me for so many summers.

Library of Congress Cataloging-in-Publication Data

Molzahn, Arlene Bourgeois.
Trucks and big rigs / Arlene Bourgeois Molzahn.
p. cm. — (Transportation & communication series)
Summary: Discusses different types of trucks, from light pickup trucks to the massive crawler-transporters that move space shuttles to the launch pad at the Kennedy Space Center in Cape Canaveral, Florida.
Includes bibliographical references and index.
ISBN 0-7660-2024-X
1. Trucks—Juvenile literature. [1. Trucks.] I. Title. II. Series.
TL230.15 .M657 2003
631.3'73—dc21 2002008921

Printed in the United States of America

10 9 8 7 6 5 4 3 2 1

To Our Readers: We have done our best to make sure all Internet Addresses in this book were active and appropriate when we went to press. However, the author and the publisher have no control over and assume no liability for the material available on those Internet sites or on other Web sites they may link to. Any comments or suggestions can be sent by e-mail to comments@enslow.com or to the address on the back cover.

Every effort has been made to locate all copyright holders of material used in this book. If any errors or omissions have occurred, corrections will be made in future editions of this book.

Illustration Credits: Sean F. Cassidy, p. 15 (bottom); Corel Corporation, pp. 24 (bottom), 25 (top), 28, 34, 36 (bottom), 37, 39; Digital Stock, a division of Corbis, pp. 10, 22, 40 (bottom); Hemera Technologies, Inc. 1997-2000, pp. 1, 2, 5, 11, 12 (top), 13 (bottom), 14, 15 (top), 17, 18 (bottom), 19 (top), 23, 24 (top), 25 (bottom), 29, 35, 41 (top); NARA, p. 20; NASA, pp. 4, 6, 7, 8, 9, 12 (bottom); Painet Stock Photos, pp. 13 (top), 16, 18 (top), 19 (bottom), 26 (top), 27, 30, 31, 33, 36 (top), 40 (top), 41 (bottom); PhotoDisc "Business and Industry", pp. 32, 38; Reality, pp. 21, 26 (bottom).

Cover Illustration: © Royalty Free/CORBIS

Contents

United States

Chapter 1

NASA's Monster Transporter

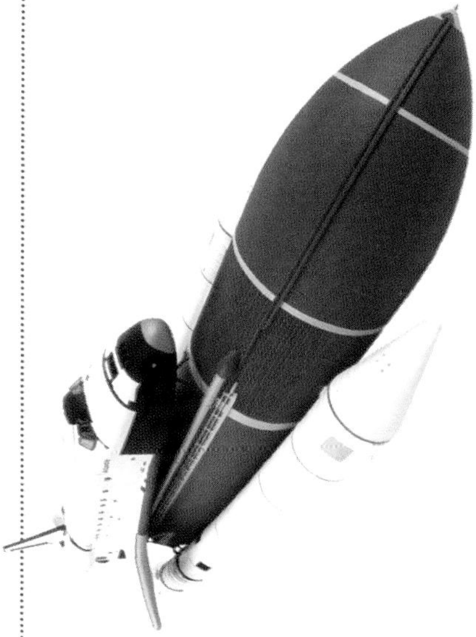

The world's largest land vehicles are the crawler-transporters at the Kennedy Space Center in Cape Canaveral, Florida. They are huge moving platforms that take space vehicles to their launchpads. The National Aeronautics and Space Administration (NASA) has two crawler-transporters.

The crawler-transporter was built to move the Apollo-Saturn V rocket. It is now used to transport the space shuttle. The space shuttle, with its booster rockets and tank, is put together in a building that is about five miles from the launchpad. This building is one of the largest in

NASA's crawler-transporters are big machines (left). This one is hauling the Space Shuttle *Endeavour* to the launchpad.

The *Apollo 11* Saturn V space vehicle lifts off.

The Vehicle Assembly Building is one of the biggest buildings in the world.

the world. The space shuttle and its launching equipment weigh almost 7,000 tons. The crawler-transporter has to be able to move this heavy load.

The crawler-transporter is 131 feet wide and 114 feet long. Its deck is about the size of a baseball infield. The transporter rides on four double tracks. These tracks are like the tracks on a tank. Each pair of these tracks is the size of a large bus.

Four diesel engines power the huge vehicle. Together these engines have over 7,600 horsepower. A family car has one engine with about 150 to 200 horsepower. The transporter must have a 400-pound grease drum changed every 11½ miles. A car must have the oil changed about every 3,000 miles. A transporter weighs 3,000 tons (about six million pounds). An average car weighs about 1½ tons or less.

The four engines on the transporter burn about 150 gallons of fuel per mile. It takes about 750 gallons of fuel to go five miles from the building where it was put together to the launchpad. It travels about one mile per hour when loaded. It can go about two miles an hour without a load.

The crawler-transporter has to be strong enough to carry the space shuttle and it's launching equipment.

It takes twelve people to operate the crawler-transporter. There are two drivers. Four people walk along the sides of the transporter and give directions on steering to the driver. Six other people are needed to help the driver. They check the gauges and watch for red warning lights. They make sure everything is working correctly as the transporter moves along.

A special roadway was built for the transporter. The base of the roadway needs to

NASA

hold the transporter and its load. The surface of the roadway is loose gravel. The transporter roadway is twelve lanes wide. That is as wide as the New Jersey Turnpike, which is the widest highway in the United States.

A company in Ohio built NASA's two crawler-transporters. They were built in Ohio and then taken apart. Then they were shipped to the Kennedy Space Center in Florida. They were put back together and were ready for use in 1967. Each transporter costs $14 million.

The two transporters are still being used today. They have traveled over 2,500 miles from the assembly building to the launchpads. NASA plans to use them for many more years.

A special roadway was built for the transporter (left).

The crawler-transporter carries the space shuttle right to the launchpad.

158
158

Chapter 2

Many Kinds of Trucks

Trucks are motor vehicles used to carry many different kinds of things. Trucks carry almost everything we eat, wear, and use. Hundreds of types of trucks are on highways hauling cargo today. There are three main kinds of trucks: light trucks, medium trucks, and heavy trucks.

Most trucks in the United States are light trucks. Most are powered by gasoline. They are called pickup trucks. Pickup trucks have a cab in front, and the back of the truck is open. This open back is called a bed. The bed is like a small box. Sometimes a cap is added to the bed. A cap has sides and a top and keeps cargo

There are many kinds of trucks, from pickups (above) to big rigs (left).

Some pickup trucks have caps on their beds. This cap protects cargo from wind, rain, and snow.

from getting wet when it rains or snows. Some pickups have a longer, or extended, cab. Trucks with extended cabs have a back seat for passengers.

Pickup trucks have many uses. Farmers use them to bring their goods to markets and to bring home supplies for their farms. Ranchers use them to bring feed and hay to their cattle. City workers who have small tools can use pickup trucks to carry their tools and supplies to work. Park rangers use pickup trucks to check campgrounds. They also

use them to bring supplies to campers.

Medium trucks are bigger and wider than light trucks. They have a cab for the driver. The back bed of a medium truck is usually closed and it looks like a large box. These trucks are used to carry medium loads for short distances. They usually have diesel engines.

Medium trucks are used by businesses that need trucks to haul goods to nearby stores. Trucking companies use them for hauling smaller loads. Furniture stores use them to deliver new furniture to homes.

Heavy trucks are the biggest and heaviest trucks on the highways. These heavy trucks are usually called big rigs. They are also called 18-wheelers or semi trucks. These trucks carry the heaviest loads. They have powerful diesel engines.

Big rigs have two separate sections. The

Farmers and ranchers use pickups to help them do their job.

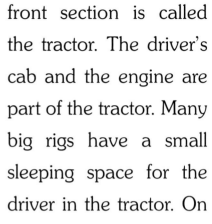

Big rigs have two separate sections. The tractor has the driver's cab and engine. The trailer is the back section of the big rig. It connects to the tractor.

front section is called the tractor. The driver's cab and the engine are part of the tractor. Many big rigs have a small sleeping space for the driver in the tractor. On long trips, a driver can pull off the highway and take a nap. Some big rigs have small refrigerators. All big rigs have cell phones or special radios so the driver can keep in contact with his or her company headquarters.

The trailer is the back section of a big rig. It is connected to the tractor. The big rig can bend where the two parts are connected. This makes it possible for long trucks to turn corners. The trailer of a big rig is usually a giant box container. The giant container can be filled with things like furniture, toys, computers, or canned goods.

In most states, big rigs must stay on main highways. They are allowed to travel on local

Trucks are sometimes used to carry furniture.

roads only when it is necessary for them to deliver their load.

There are many special kinds of trucks. Bookmobiles are libraries on wheels. Ambulances are special trucks with lifesaving equipment that rush people to hospitals. Fire trucks are always ready to race to put out fires. Refrigerator trucks make it possible for people to have fresh fruit and vegetables all year.

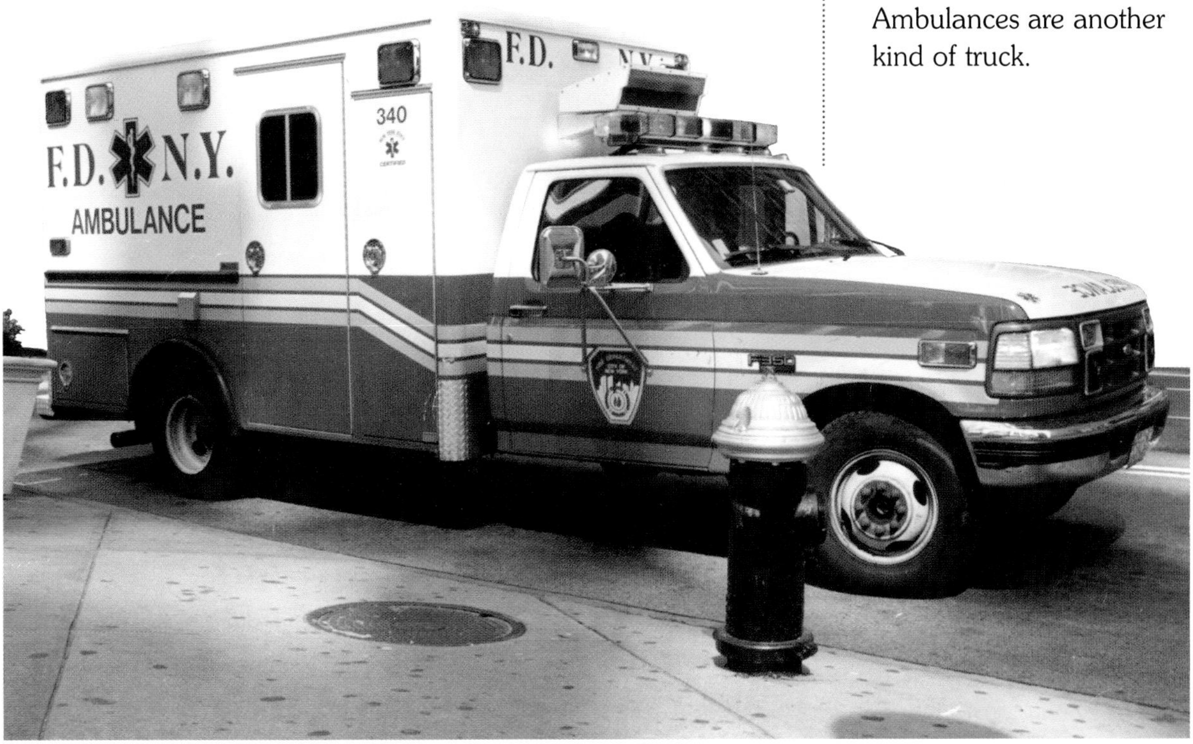

Ambulances are another kind of truck.

HUNT
OLIVER
CONTADINA

CARTER DAIRY

Chapter 3

Early Trucks

No one knows for sure who made the first successful truck. By the mid-1890s, trucks were being built in the United States. The first truck company in the United States was in Philadelphia, Pennsylvania. These trucks were different from the trucks we have today. They did not have cabs for the drivers. The drivers sat on a seat in the open air. The trucks had solid rubber tires. They traveled on narrow bumpy roads. The trucks and their cargo were nearly shaken apart as they traveled on these rough roads. Truck driving was not an easy job.

People could not depend on trucks. The

Trucks from long ago did not have cabs or closed trailers. Drivers sat out in the open (top left). These children play on the back of an old dairy truck (bottom left).

trucks broke down often. Without refrigeration, milk and groceries spoiled quickly. So horses and wagons were still used to carry these products for many years after the truck was invented.

Trucks slowly improved and were used to deliver goods.

There were about 700 trucks in the United States by 1904. Most trucks weighed more than the loads they carried. They did not have starters in the cab. They were started by turning a crank handle in front of the truck. After the engine started, the driver hurried into the driver's seat and began to steer the truck.

As trucks improved, they were used to carry loads for long distances. In 1911, the first truck was successfully driven across the United States. Trucks did not travel very fast in those days and roads were very poor. So, it took the trucker sixty days.

After World War I, cabs were built on the trucks so that the driver did not have to sit in the open air. Tires were improved. The first tires for army vehicles were made of steel. Later, tires were made of solid rubber. After the war, air-filled rubber tires were used on trucks and cars, which made riding in these vehicles a lot smoother.

Better engines were built so that trucks could go faster and carry heavier loads.

By the 1920s and the 1930s trucks were used to deliver milk and bread.

USA
72264-S
B-9
82 A/B
307 L

Windowpanes were put in the cabs, and later windshield wipers were invented. Safety glass was another great improvement. It prevented the driver and passengers from being cut from broken glass during an accident. Later, heaters and air conditioning made traveling more comfortable. Today, people are still working to improve trucks and big rigs.

Many kinds of trucks were used during World War II in 1945 (left).

Today truck engines are built to be faster and carry heavier loads.

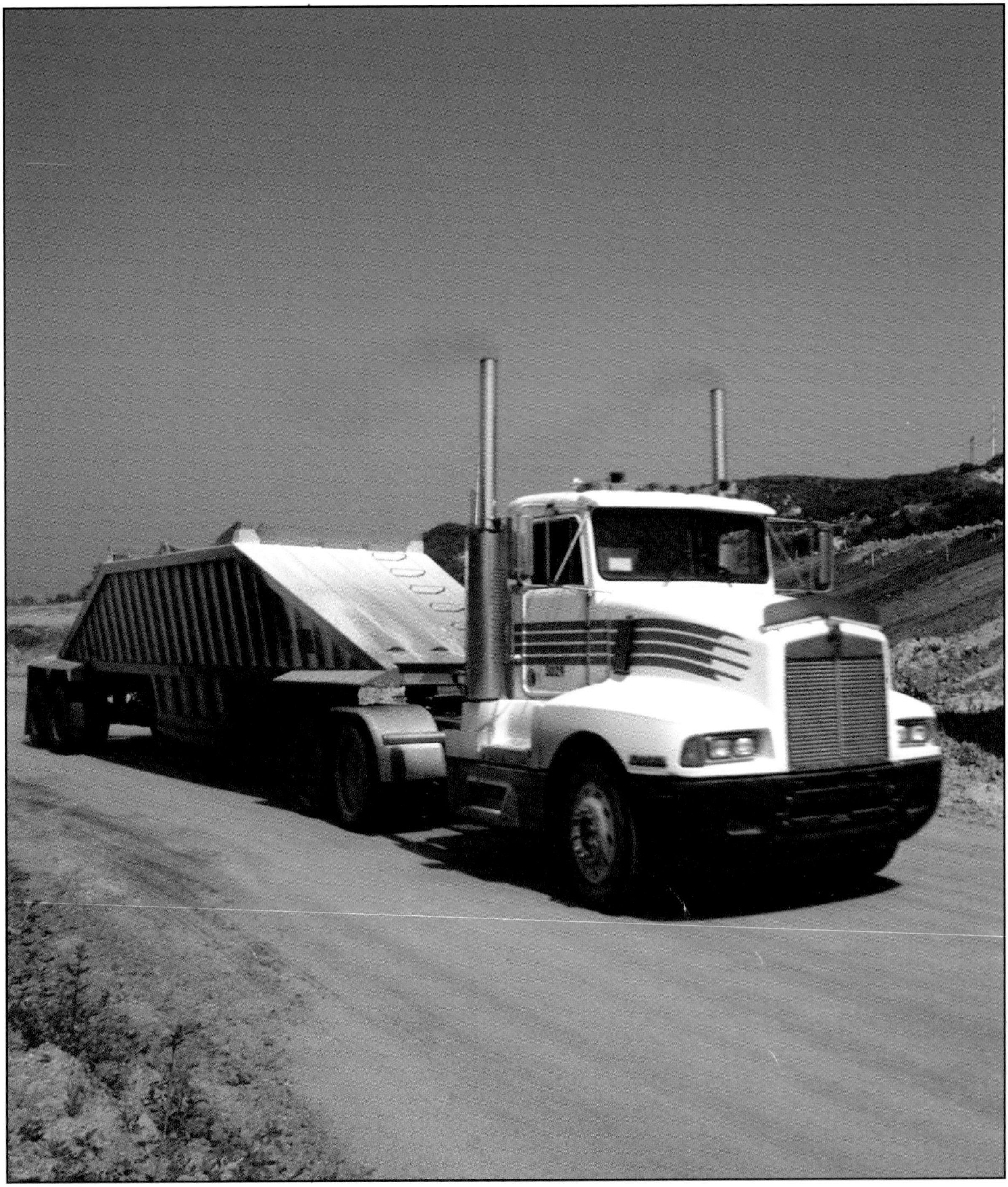

Chapter 4

All Kinds of Big Rigs

Big rigs come in different shapes and sizes (left).

Big rigs are built to haul many different kinds of cargo. There is a trailer built to haul almost any kind of load.

Big rigs carry parts for cars that are made in several different cities. These parts must all be trucked to a main factory where the cars are put together. After the cars are finished, they are put on big rigs called car transporters. Car transporters carry the cars to car dealers all over the United States. The cars are driven on and off the transporter using a ramp.

Some big rigs drive on logging roads to pick up loads of logs. These big rigs have an open

There are special trucks that carry logs to lumber mills.

trailer with side rails. Large chains or cables keep the logs in place on the trailer. The logs are brought to lumber mills where they are sawed into boards.

Some big rigs have a large tank for a trailer. These big rigs are called tankers. The inside of the tanker is divided into sections. Liquids like gasoline and heating oil are carried in tankers. Gasoline and other fuels can be very

Tanker trucks can carry liquids from milk to heating oil.

dangerous. Special signs on all four sides of the tanker tell firefighters and police officers what is inside. Then, in case of an accident, they know what to do if the liquid is spilled. A refrigerated tanker truck brings milk from farms to cheese factories or to milk bottling plants.

Special trailers are made to carry cattle, sheep, and hogs. These trailers have several sections in them so that the animals cannot move around. They also have many holes in

Cattle and other animals can be carried in special trailers.

the sides of the trailer so that the animals can breathe.

Sometimes big rigs have to carry very wide or odd-shaped cargo. These loads are carried on a flatbed and are called oversize loads. Houses, large boats, and construction equipment all need to be loaded on a flatbed trailer. When a big rig is carrying an oversize load, it travels very slowly. Cars with flashing lights travel in front and in back of the big rig. These cars warn drivers to be careful of the slow moving vehicle with an oversize load.

In Australia, where cities are very far apart, road train trucks are used. A road train is a truck that pulls from two to four trailers at the same time. The trailers are joined together so they

Oversize loads are carried on special trailers. The cab has a sign on the front so that other drivers know there is an oversize load.

can bend for curves in the highway. Road train trucks are not allowed to go into cities. They must load and unload their cargo at special places outside the city. In some western parts of the United States, trucks are allowed to pull two or three trailers. These are called longer combination vehicles (LCVs).

This road train has three trailers. Road trains are used in Australia because the cities are so far apart.

ECYCLING SERVICES
SKT283
SK 293

Chapter 5

Many, Many Jobs

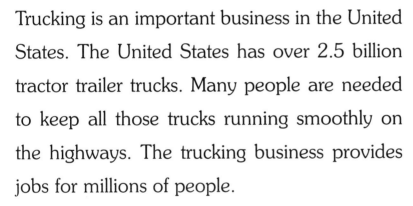

Trucking is an important business in the United States. The United States has over 2.5 billion tractor trailer trucks. Many people are needed to keep all those trucks running smoothly on the highways. The trucking business provides jobs for millions of people.

Truck drivers must be very good drivers. Driving a big rig around corners or backing them into parking spaces is not easy. Truckers travel at high speeds. A driver's mistake can cause an accident or a chain of accidents on a busy freeway. So a truck driver needs to go to a truck driving school.

Trucking is big business in the United States and many other countries. The goods we see on store shelves might have been delivered by a big rig.

People go to school to be truck drivers. These women are learning about different parts of an engine.

Trucking companies need many people to keep the business running.

At truck driving school, drivers spend several weeks in a classroom learning the rules of the road. They learn the special skills needed to become a truck driver. After the classroom work, the students spend two to three months in a learning truck. A teacher sits next to the driver in the learning truck. At first the new driver drives the truck in areas where there is very little traffic. Later, he or she drives the truck in heavy city traffic.

After a driver has finished driving school, he or she must take a written driving test. He or she must also take a driver's test using a big rig in city traffic. Drivers must pass both tests before they can get a license to drive a truck. Many teachers have jobs helping truck drivers get their licenses.

Trucking companies hire many office workers. Trucks have computers, cell phones, and some even have fax machines in them. When a driver has reached the end of a route, people at the trucking company tell the driver where to go for a new load. Trucking companies hire many people to keep in touch with the drivers. They also need computer programmers, shipping clerks, and payroll clerks.

Trucking companies hire many mechanics. Mechanics keep trucks in good driving condition and make necessary repairs.

Many workers are needed to load and unload trucks. Companies who help people move from one place to another also have packers. Packers are workers who carefully pack a family's belongings that are to be moved.

Truck manufacturing companies hire many factory workers to build new trucks. They also hire engineers to help design new trucks. Truck companies are always looking for ways

Everyone plays an important role in the company.

Mechanics make sure the trucks work well.

to make trucks safer. They also want to build trucks that need fewer repairs and that use less fuel.

Many different companies make parts for trucks. Some companies make engines and others make trailers. Still others make the electrical equipment that truckers need to keep in touch with their company headquarters. Other companies make things for the inside of the cab, like the seats and the small bed for the driver. Every tractor trailer uses at least sixteen tires, so trucking companies buy a lot of tires.

Truckers bring business to service stations and restaurants along the highways. There are places where truckers can stop and take a shower along their route. All of these places need workers to help run their businesses.

Truck companies are always looking for ways to have safe trucks on the highway (left).

Rest areas are places where truck drivers can rest. Some rest areas have restaurants and places where truck drivers can take showers.

Chapter 6

Trucks for Today and Tomorrow

Trucks are a very important part of our transportation system. Nearly 65% of all the products in the United States are moved by truck. Trucking companies in the United States earn over $600 billion a year. Trucking is important in almost every major country in the world.

Sometimes trucks and ships work together to move goods around the world. Products are packed in huge boxes on big rig trailers. These huge boxes are called containers. Big rigs bring these containers to the docks. Then these containers are disconnected from the trailer

Trucks and ships work together to deliver products all over the world (left).

and a crane lifts them onto a ship. The ship brings the containers to the right port. There they are unloaded and put on big rig trucks to be hauled to stores.

When trucks and trains get together to move cargo, it is called piggybacking. Sometimes a loaded trailer is unhooked from the tractor and is loaded onto a railroad flatcar. The train then moves the trailer to the correct railroad yard.

The containers below were just brought in by a ship. They will be moved from a ship to a trailer. The big rig will deliver the container.

There the trailer is unloaded and reconnected to another truck tractor so the goods can be delivered.

The federal, state, and city governments in the United States use more trucks than any other industry. The United States armed forces use many different kinds of trucks to carry equipment, troops, weapons, and supplies. Trucks are used to deliver mail. State governments use trucks to build and take care of parks, bridges, and roads. Cities have special trucks for the police, fire, and park departments. Trucks are used to sweep streets, to plow snow, and to collect garbage.

Truckers and the trucking industry in the United States have many rules that they must follow. Congress passed the Motor Carrier Act of 1935 to help control interstate trucking. This law made sure that the rules for truckers were the same from one state

Above is a Black Hawk helicopter carrying a truck used by the United States armed forces. Snow plows (bottom) keep roads clear after a snow storm.

Congress passed laws to protect truck drivers.

to another. Congress passed the Motor Carrier Act of 1980 to help the trucking industry. The law changed some of the rules for certain types of trucks.

Safety is the most important thing when driving a big rig. Tired drivers can cause serious accidents on the highways. Drivers are not allowed to drive more than sixty hours a week. After driving for ten straight hours, they must take off eight hours to rest. Drivers must keep a record showing the hours they drove and the hours they rested. They must make sure their trucks are in good working condition.

Safety is very important when driving a big rig. These firefighters are in gear to protect themselves. Chemicals spilled out of the tanker after an accident.

Many years ago, only men were truck drivers. Today anyone can be one.

Truck manufacturers are working hard to make trucks safer and easier to drive. They are also trying to streamline their trucks and trailers. A sleek, smooth vehicle cuts down the amount of air through which the truck must travel. This will save fuel because the engine will not have to work as hard. New

super-sleek trucks will be on the highways soon.

Trucking companies in the United States pay a lot of taxes. This tax money is used to fix highways and to build new ones.

Many years ago, only men were truck drivers. Today both men and women are hired by trucking companies to drive trucks. These men and women help to make our lives better by bringing food and goods from all over the world to cities and towns.

Truck drivers make sure goods are delivered all over the world. They load and unload their cargo. Many items are brought to places by trucks and big rigs.

Timeline

1890s—Trucks are being built in the United States.

1900s—Air-filled tires and gasoline engines let trucks carry heavier loads at greater speeds.

1904—There are about 700 trucks in use in the United States.

1911—The first truck is driven across the United States.

1917–1918—Great improvements are made on trucks for World War I.

1920s—Building of a national system of highways begins. Better roads let trucks travel quickly between cities.

Timeline

1935—Congress passes the Motor Carrier Act of 1935, which gives the Interstate Commerce Commission the ability to regulate big rigs and drivers traveling from state to state.

1980—Congress passes the Motor Carrier Act of 1980, which lessens some restrictions on types of carriers.

2002—There are over 2.5 billion tractor trailer trucks in use in the United States.

Words to Know

cab—The place where the driver sits in a truck.

diesel fuel—A type of fuel used in most trucks and big rigs.

interstate—Any business or traveling done between two or more states.

license—The right given by law to do something. A driver's license gives a person the right to drive a car.

longer combination vehicles (LCVs)—A truck pulling two or three trailers; the American term for road train.

mechanic—A worker who checks over machinery and makes repairs when needed.

oversize—A size larger than the usual or proper size.

piggybacking—When loaded truck trailers are put on railroad flatcars and move to another railroad yard.

Words to Know

road train—An Australian term for a truck with more than one trailer. Some road trains have many trailers.

sleek—Having a smooth form with no sharp corners.

streamline—Having a smooth, flowing shape.

tanker—A ship or a tank truck that is used to carry liquids.

Learn More About Trucks and Big Rigs

Books

Bledsoe, Glen and Karen E. Bledsoe. *The World's Fastest Trucks*. Mankato, Minn.: Capstone Press, Inc., 2002.

Froeb, Lori. *Trucks at Work*. Pleasantville, N.Y.: Reader's Digest Children's Publishing, Inc., 2002.

Jango-Cohen, Judith. *Dump Trucks*. Minneapolis, Minn.: Lerner Publishing Group, 2003.

Milton, Joyce. *Heavy Duty Trucks*. Madison, Wisc.: Turtleback Books, 2000.

Simon, Seymour. *Seymour Simon's Book of Trucks*. New York: HarperCollins, 2000.

Stille, Darlene. *Big Rigs*. Minneapolis, Minn.: Compass Point Books, 2002.

Learn More About Trucks and Big Rigs

Internet Addresses

Crawler-Transporter

<http://science.ksc.nasa.gov/facilities/crawler.html>

Learn more about NASA's crawler-transporter.

The Great Sparky the Fire Dog

<http://www.nfpa.org/sparky/>

This is a great site from the National Fire Protection Association. Click on "Fun with Fire Trucks" and learn more!

Index

ICCRX +
631
.373
M